PIRATES!

Saviour Pirotta

Wayland

Pirates!

Volcanoes and Earthquakes

Editor: Sarah Doughty
Cover design: Giles Wheeler

Published in 1998 by
Wayland Publishers Ltd
61 Western Road, Hove
East Sussex, BN3 1JD

British Library Cataloguing in Publication Data
Pirotta, Saviour
    Pirates! - (Amazing World)
    1. Pirates - Juvenile literature
    I. Title
    364.1'64

ISBN 0 7502 2269 7

Printed and bound in Italy by G. Canale & C. S.p.A.

This book is based on *Pirates and Treasure* by the same
author published in 1996 by Wayland Publishers Ltd.

Picture acknowledgements
AKG, Berlin 4 (bottom); Bridgeman Art Library, London
24 (bottom)/Private Collection, 44 (bottom)/National
Maritime Museum, London; C M Dixon 17 (bottom), 18
(right); Mary Evans Picture Library 18 (left), 36 (and
cover), 45; Eye Ubiquitous 26 (bottom)/P B Adams, 44
(top)/John Dakers; Michael Holford 9 (bottom); Ann
Ronan at Image Select 8 (centre); National Maritime
Museum, London title page, 11 (bottom), 14, 15, 33 (top),
34 (bottom), 38-9, 40, 42 (bottom); Peter Newark's
Historical Pictures 4 (top), 7, 11 (top), 16 (bottom), 19,
(bottom), 23 (bottom), 24 (top), 25 (bottom), 26 (top),
27, 28 (and cover), 30, 31 (top), 31 (bottom), 33
(bottom), 34 (top), 34-5, 37 (bottom), 40-41, 41, 46 (top
left), 46 (bottom right); Ronald Sheridan's Photo
Library/Ancient Art and Architecture Collection 6, 8
(left), 13, 16 (top), 22 (centre), 23 (top), 25 (top), 42
(top); Wayland Picture Library 9 (top), 20 (top), 20
(bottom), 21 (top), 46 (bottom left).

The maps, flags and other artwork on pages 4, 5, 9, 10, 12,
17, 18 (top), 19 (top), 21 (bottom), 22, 29 (top and
bottom), 32, 37 (top), 38, 39 (bottom), 43 and 46 (top
centre and top right) are by Barbara Loftus.

Contents

What is a Pirate?

Pirates were robbers who sailed the high seas. Armed with swords and pistols, they attacked passing ships and made off with the booty.

▼ Many people considered pirates to be daring and handsome. Film actors like Errol Flynn became famous playing sea robbers.

▲ Cunning pirates often dressed up as women to lure passing ships into coming closer.

No one was safe from the pirates. They operated in every sea around the world and most of the rivers too. Some pirates were born criminals. Others started out as honest men but became pirates later on in life. Writers, doctors, soldiers, even bishops became pirates.

Most honest sailors remained poor all their lives but pirates could become rich overnight. Nearly all pirates were rogues. But many of them were brave too. Their ships were often smaller than the ones they attacked. And they carried fewer men.

▼ Most pirates sailed in the busy trade routes where they could attack lots of treasure-laden ships.

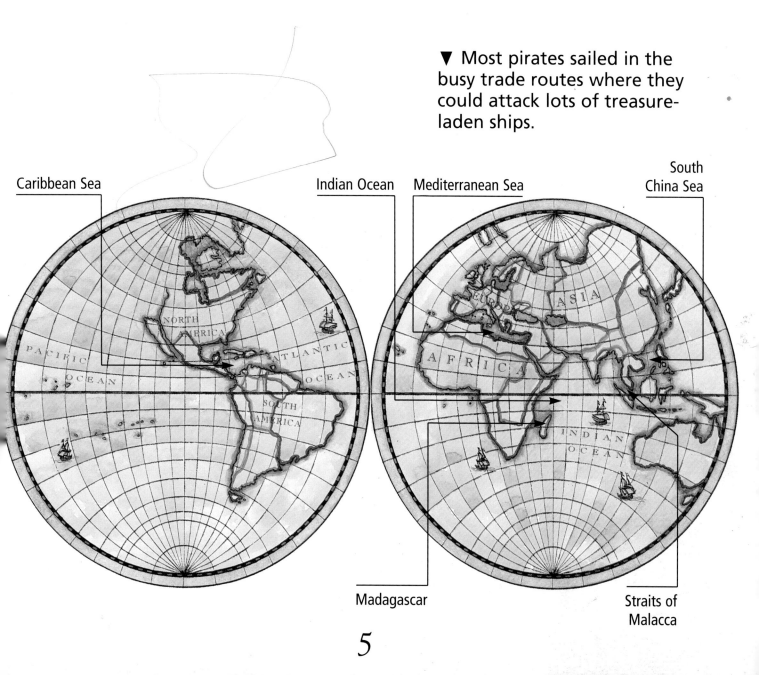

Caribbean Sea

Indian Ocean

Mediterranean Sea

South China Sea

NORTH AMERICA

PACIFIC OCEAN

ATLANTIC OCEAN

SOUTH AMERICA

EUROPE

ASIA

AFRICA

INDIAN OCEAN

Madagascar

Straits of Malacca

Some kings and queens hired pirates to attack the ships of other countries. The pirates were give a written permit and called themselves 'privateers' to distinguish them from other sea robbers.

The first pirates

Some of the world's earliest sailors were also pirates. The Phoenicians, who sailed around the Mediterranean around 2000 BC, attacked ships and coastal towns. They kidnapped people and sold them off as slaves.

Around 150 BC, some pirates started to operate along the south eastern coast of Turkey, a region which was then called Cilicia. They ransacked Roman ships and stole grain bound from Egypt to Rome.

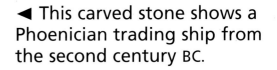

◄ This carved stone shows a Phoenician trading ship from the second century BC.

Caesar's ransom

Around 75 BC, a young man called Julius Caesar was going to Rhodes for his summer holidays. On the way, his ship was captured by pirates. One of the robbers recognized Caesar. He convinced his mates that they should hold him to ransom.

'How much money are you going to ask for?' demanded Caesar. '20 talents of gold,' said the pirates. Caesar was angry. 'I am going to be the emperor of Rome one day,' he bellowed. 'I am worth at least 50 talents.' The pirates asked Caesar's family for 50 talents. The money was sent right away.

But the pirates did not live to enjoy it. When Caesar was freed, he hunted them down and had them all killed.

▲ Many people believe that the pirates forced their victims to 'walk the plank'.In fact, no one knows if it really happened.

The Cilician (Turkish) pirates became rich and powerful. By 67 BC they had captured some 400 cities. So the Romans sent a general called Pompey to crush them once and for all.

▼ Cilician pirates celebrate another victory with food and wine.

Pompey chased the pirates until he had captured them all. But he didn't kill them. Instead he gave them some land where they could start a new life as farmers.

▲ A Roman coin shows Pompey's head.

Who were the Corsairs?

► Christians became pirates during the wars against the Muslims.

▼ The battle of Lepanto was the last great battle between Christian and Muslim pirates. It took place on the 7 October 1571. The Christians won.

In the first half of the seventh century, the Prophet Muhammad founded a religion called Islam. The followers of Islam are called Muslim. The new faith spread quickly throughout the Arab countries.

This did not go down well in Europe. Many Christians were angry that the 'Holy Land' where Jesus had lived was in Muslim hands. They were also worried that Islam might wipe out their own way of life.

▲ By the sixteenth century, Muslim pirates had caused mayhem all around the Mediterranean Sea. The island of Malta became the base for many Christian pirates.

Years of bloodshed followed as Christians and Muslims fought for control over the Mediterranean Sea and the countries around it. The fighting produced a new kind of pirate: the corsair.

The Corsairs

Christian corsairs were employed by Christian governments. They attacked Muslim galleys in order to weaken their enemies. Many of them worked for the Knights of Saint John, a military order of Christian Knights.

The Muslim corsairs gave a share of their booty to the Deys, the military leaders of Muslim countries.

The corsair's favourite booty was people. Rich men were ransomed. Poorer folk were sold off as slaves in the markets of North Africa.

Slaves bought for rowing in the galleys did not survive long. They had to work all day and night and were given very little to eat.

Slaves not bought by private owners became the property of the local government. They were made to work at hard jobs, like quarrying, often with a ball and chain fixed to one leg.

▲ Muslim pirates forced their Christian slaves to row all day and night.

◀ Some slaves tried to escape from Muslim galleys in boats. Many died from thirst.

Corsair Galleys

The ships used by the corsairs were called galleys. Muslim galleys were usually 55 m long and 5 m wide. During battle they were propelled by oarsmen.

▲ Muslim galleys were driven by oarsmen as well as sails.

Muslims captured by Christians were also treated badly. Many were taken to the slave market in Malta and sold. In the seventeenth century many European pirates joined the Muslim corsairs so they could get more booty. They taught the Arabs a lot about ships.

A Muslim galley usually had only one mast and one cannon. Muslim pirates relied on their skills as swordsmen to win battles.

Christian galleys had three masts. They had more cannons too. Christian pirates preferred gun battle to sword fights. Some of them were incredibly skilled gunmen.

The hulls of all galleys needed regular scraping and waxing to keep them smooth. This meant the ships could cut through the water easily.

▲ The Pope's own heavily-armed galley.

Simon Danzinger

A Christian pirate, Simon Danziger, showed the Muslim corsairs how to build stronger ships like the Northern Europeans. With these, the corsairs could venture out of the Mediterranean Sea and attack countries like England, Ireland and Iceland.

◀ Aruj and Kheir-ed-din were the most feared Muslim pirates in the world.

The Barbarossa Brothers

In the first half of the sixteenth century, the Barbarossa brothers were the most famous corsairs in the Mediterranean.

They were called Aruj and Kheir-ed-din. In 1504 Aruj captured two ships belonging to the Pope. The Christians were livid.

Some years later the Dey of Algiers asked for the brothers' help. The Spanish had built a fort on the coast of his country and his pirates couldn't sail in and out. Could the Barbarossas help him to destroy the fort?

Aruj attacked the fort. But he could not destroy it. Then his pirates started fighting between themselves. Some even attacked Algerian corsairs.

The Dey was shocked. He realized that the Spanish were much less dangerous than the Barbarossas and he asked them to help destroy the brothers.
The Spanish agreed. But the Barbarossas seized a city and started attacking any ship that came their way. The Spanish got angry. They sent 10,000 soldiers to get rid of the brothers.

As the galleons approached the city, the Barbarossas fled with their gold. They were captured trying to cross a river. Aruj was killed. But Kheir-ed-din escaped. Later he became the leader of a Turkish fleet and made it the finest in the world. It is said that he lived in splendour well into old age.

▼ Spanish galleons were often attacked by pirates as they tried to reach their bases in Italy.

◄ Dragut Rais

Grapes for Dragut

Dragut Rais worked for the Barbarossa brothers. He was very cruel. The Maltese say that he once sent a young pirate to fetch him some grapes from a field on the island.

The pirate swam ashore and returned with a bunch. But Dragut realized that the stalk was broken. He was very angry. He had the poor pirate taken back to the grape field and burned alive.

▼ A US navy ship attacks a Muslim galley. The Americans hated paying bribes to the pirates and swore to destroy them.

During the eighteenth century many Muslim countries fell under European control. The corsairs began to disappear. The Deys gave up piracy and so did the Christians. A wild and dangerous era had come to an end.

Where was the Spanish Main?

▼ The Spanish did not want other Europeans to trade with their colonies.

In 1523, a French pirate called Jean Florin and his crew attacked three Spanish ships near Portugal.

They got away with three chests full of gold, lots of emeralds, pearls and gold dust.

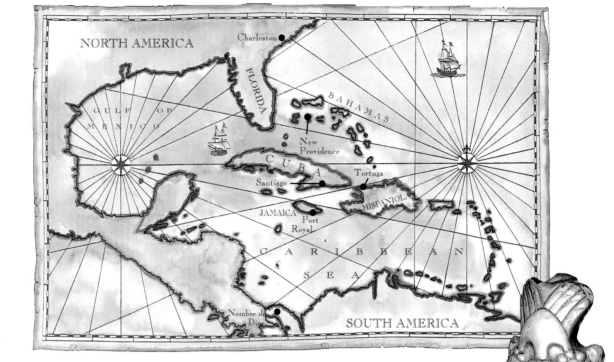

▲ The Spanish Main consisted of the American mainland, the West Indies, the Gulf of Mexico and the Caribbean with all its islands.

◄ Spanish soldiers load treasure on to a ship.

► All the silver and gold pouring into Spain made other countries jealous.

The Spanish were furious. Since Christopher Columbus had reached America in 1492, they had filled one ship after another with gold stolen from the local people. And they insisted on keeping the Spanish Main to themselves.

Privateers

So the French and the English sent pirates called privateers to ransack Spanish ships on their way home.

They were called privateers to distinguish them from ordinary sea robbers.

The privateers gave most of their Spanish booty to the kings and queens who employed them. Even so, they became very rich.

Soon Spanish ships started travelling together for safety. So the privateers began attacking Spanish ports instead.

▲ A Spanish galleon.

Pegleg

Francois Le Clerk was a French privateer. People called him Pie de Palo, or Pegleg, because he had a wooden leg.

The most famous disabled pirate in the world is Long John Silver who stars in the famous book *Treasure Island* by R.L Stevenson. In a film of the book the pirate was played by actor Robert Newton.

Francis Drake

Francis Drake was the most famous English privateer. He first went to sea with his cousin John Hawkins. Hawkins was a slave trader. But when Drake went to sea on his own, he became a privateer.

▲ Queen Elizabeth I hated the Spanish. She hired privateers to attack Spanish ships.

One day he brought Queen Elizabeth I £30,000 worth of booty. He made £10,000 out of that expedition. Drake's dream was to capture the famous city of Nombre de Dios in Panama, which is where the Spanish kept most of their gold.

► Sir Francis Drake, Queen Elizabeth I's main privateer, sailed the world on the *Golden Hind.*

Drake's first attack went wrong. He was shot in the leg and had to turn back. Then he heard that a mule train was coming to Nombre de Dios laden with gold. His men tried to attack that. This time he succeeded. It was the first of many successful raids.

The Queen was so pleased with Drake she made him a knight and gave him a special sword.

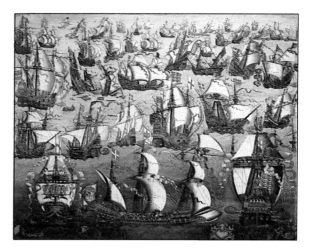

▲ The Spanish Armada was a fleet of ships sent by the king of Spain to England to stop the looting of Spanish ships.

Code of Conduct

Many pirates lived by a code of conduct similar to that of the privateers. Here are some of the rules they had to obey:

- The captain was entitled to one full share and a half of the booty.
- Men caught stealing from the ship's coffers had their noses slit and were marooned on a desert island.
- Anyone who tried to desert the ship was executed.
- No one was allowed to leave the ship until there was at least £1,000 worth of booty on it.
- Candles had to be blown out by 8 pm sharp.
- Anyone who wanted to keep on drinking after that time had to do it on deck, by moonlight.
- Musicians were hired to play music during attacks. Musicians were allowed Sundays off.

Who were the Buccaneers?

▲ A buccaneer hunts for pigs on the island of Hispaniola. He carries a musket and has a dog.

In 1630, Spain allowed France and England to settle in parts of the Spanish Main. This put many privateers out of a job.

Buccaneers

Some drifted to the Caribbean island of Hispaniola. They made friends with the Arawaks who lived there. The Arawaks showed them how to barbecue pigs on an open fire called *boucan*. This meal soon became the men's favourite dish. People began to call them buccaneers, after the dish.

Someone had the idea of selling barbecued pig to passing sailors. The Spanish would have none of it. They attacked Hispaniola and killed all the pigs. The buccaneers escaped to Tortuga, a small island off the coast of Hispaniola.

The Brethren of the Coast

The buccaneers were so angry that they attacked a Spanish galleon and made off with the gold. Soon all the buccaneers turned into pirates. They called themselves the Brethren of the Coast. Tortuga became their headquarters.

The buccaneers tried to treat everyone fairly. Before a raid, they met to discuss plans. The captain welcomed suggestions from everyone.

▼ A buccaneer on a lookout for ships.

▼ The pirates always shared out the booty straight after a raid. Some retired to live on the proceeds. Many spent their share right away.

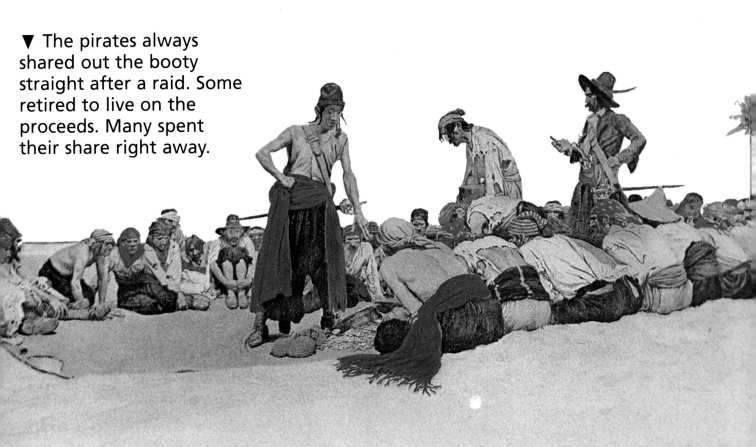

23

▲ The buccaneers often crept up on Spanish galleons in small boats called pinnaces. They attacked without warning.

Many buccaneers had 'free insurance' against bodily harm. Men who lost their right hand were given 600 pieces of eight (silver coins). Men who lost their left arm got 500.

As the buccaneers grew in numbers, they moved from Tortuga to Jamaica. Jamaica had been captured by the British from the Spanish.

The British liked having the pirates there. They knew the Spanish would not dare to attack them as long as the harbour was full of pirate ships. They even gave the buccaneers permission to attack the Spanish galleons.

► Pirates swarming aboard a Spanish galleon. They were after gold and anything useful, like ropes, medicine and food.

The treasures seized from the Spanish included silver, gold, pearls, emeralds and pieces of eight.

Linen, velvet, wine, brandy and preserved foods were all considered as valuable as gold. In 1630, Captain John Smith described the haul taken by pirates from a Venetian merchant ship. It included silk, gold cloth, gold and silver.

In the last years of the seventeenth century, Spain lost much of its power and land around the Caribbean.

▲ Some Spanish treasure chests had complicated locks.

► The Dutch pirate Rock Brasiliano roasted his captives alive.

Henry Morgan (c.1635-1688)

Henry Morgan was born in Wales. In his teens he joined a pirate ship on its way to Tortuga. There he became a buccaneer. Morgan and his new friends soon had enough gold to kit out their own pirate ship. He was made captain of the first raid. It was a success. More raids followed.

Soon Morgan was made Vice-Admiral of the buccaneer fleet. He became very rich. He bought a plantation and employed many slaves. The governor of Jamaica gave Morgan permission to attack Spanish ships on behalf of the English. Morgan sailed to Panama and attacked the Spanish city of Portobello.

He returned to Jamaica with lots of treasure and 300 slaves. Morgan then raided the city of Maracaibo on the coast. of Venezuela. But the way out of the harbour was blocked by enemy ships. Morgan acted quickly. He filled a captured ship with tar and sulphur. He crammed the decks with kegs of gunpowder. His men made fake cannons out of Indian

So there were fewer ships to attack. Besides, many countries began to rely more on their navies. They had no more use for privateers. The days of Caribbean buccaneering seemed to be over.

► Blackbeard's castle still stands on Saint Thomas in the Virgin Islands.

drums. Dummy pirates with pumpkins for heads were put by the rigging. A dummy of Morgan himself was planted on the quarterdeck.

Then a handful of men steered the ship towards the Spanish galleons. When it was close, they lit the fuses to the kegs and escaped in small boats. A few minutes later the Spanish fired. The ship blew up. So did the Spanish galleons. There was a battle and Morgan managed to escape.

▶ Henry Morgan's buccaneers raided the town of Panama in 1670.

In 1701 Spain, England and France were at war. When the fighting ended in 1713, many sailors found themselves out of a job and penniless. Some chose to earn a living by taking up piracy.

Blackbeard
One group of Caribbean pirates was led by Blackbeard.

▲ Blackbeard put lighted tapers in his hair to frighten the enemy.

Blackbeard was perhaps the most infamous pirate that ever lived. His real name was probably Edward Teach. He was born in Bristol around 1680 and started his career as a privateer. Then he joined a pirate ship.

The ship's captain soon noticed Blackbeard had talent: when he wanted to get a ring from a victim he didn't bother asking for it. He just chopped off the finger and dropped it in his pocket. When the pirates captured a large French ship, Blackbeard made it his own. He called it *Queen Anne's Revenge*.

By this time the pirates had enough treasure to last them a lifetime. But Blackbeard went on looting. He even held the American city of Charleston in South Carolina to ransom. Soon Blackbeard's men became fed up with the sea. They wanted to go ashore and spend some of their loot.

So they sailed to Bath in North Carolina and asked for the Royal Pardon. That meant the king would forgive them their crimes if they promised to stop looting. The pardon was granted.

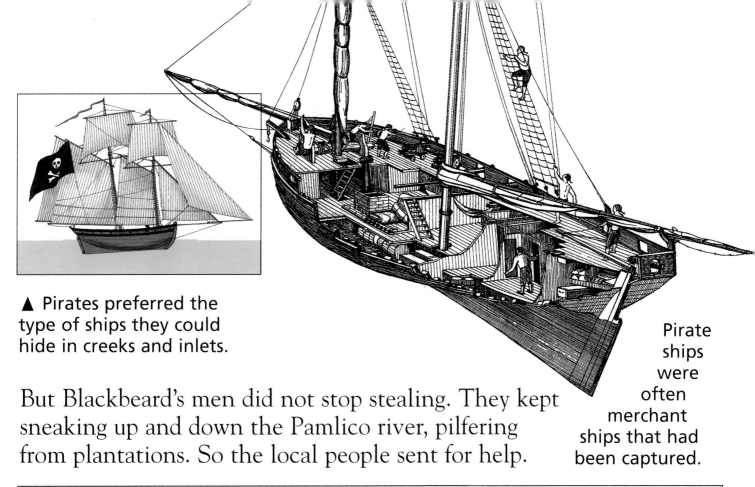

▲ Pirates preferred the type of ships they could hide in creeks and inlets.

Pirate ships were often merchant ships that had been captured.

But Blackbeard's men did not stop stealing. They kept sneaking up and down the Pamlico river, pilfering from plantations. So the local people sent for help.

The Jolly Roger

The words Jolly Roger come from the French Joli Rouge, which means 'pretty red'. Pirates who intended to kill all their victims flew a blood red flag from their mast. Later, many famous pirates had their own flags. Blackbeard's showed a skeleton holding an hourglass and a spear, piercing the heart.

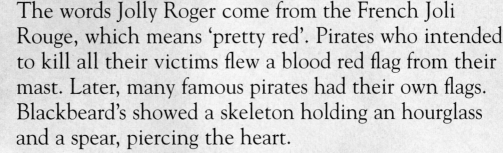

◄ These are the flags of Christopher Condent, Blackbeard, Thomas Tew, Calico Jack and Stede Bonnet. The red flag was used by Muslim corsairs.

The British Navy sent Lieutenant Robert Maynard to wipe out Blackbeard's gang. He tracked them down to their lair in Ocracoke Inlet in Pamlico Sound.

Most of Blackbeard's men were killed. But Blackbeard kept on fighting till he was brought down by 20 cutlass (sword) wounds and five gunshots.

Mary Read and Anne Bonny

Mary Read

Mary Read and Anne Bonny both sailed the seas dressed as men. Mary was born in Plymouth in 1690. She became a pirate, pretending she was a boy. When King George I gave a pardon to all pirates, Mary gave up the sea. But she soon ran out of loot. So she joined the ship of a famous pirate called Calico Jack, named after his brightly coloured calico clothes.

30

Thirteen of the pirates who survived were hanged. It was the beginning of the end for pirates in the Caribbean. The navy hunted most of them down.

Besides, there were two new places for pirates to haunt: the Indian Ocean and the China Sea.

◄ When Blackbeard was killed, his head was hung from the prow of a ship.

Anne Bonny

There she met Anne Bonny, who was Calico Jack's girlfriend. Anne and Mary became friends. In 1720 their pirate ship was captured. Most of the crew were sent to the gallows. But Anne and Mary claimed they were pregnant. So they were sent to prison instead where Mary died. Anne was never heard of again.

Where did the Buccaneers go?

When the buccaneers first went to the Indian Ocean they discovered that it was full of local pirates such as the Gujurati pirates. Some of them had been robbing there for hundreds of years. They were very cruel and they stopped at nothing to lay their hands on gold and jewels.

The Gujurati pirates used to make their victims drink a mixture of sea water and tamarind (a fruit). The horrible drink made the prisoners sick. The pirates would then look through the vomit to see if the merchants had swallowed any pearls or precious stones.

◄ Piracy in the Indian Ocean still goes on to this very day.

Vasco da Gama

In 1497, a Portuguese explorer called Vasco da Gama sailed into the Indian Ocean. da Gama was a Christian. He saw no harm in robbing the ships of people who did not believe in the Christian faith. Many European traders followed in his wake, robbing and looting the ships of non-Christians.

Soon the ocean was seething with pirates. Merchant ships stole booty from local people, pirates and other European traders. By the sixteenth century, the situation had become so bad that the emperor of India asked Britain and Holland to get rid of the pirates.

▲ Vasco da Gama loved looting ships. He was also the target of local pirates himself.

A company called the British East India company tried very hard to clear the ocean.

◀ A British trading ship setting off to stamp out piracy in the Indian Ocean.

▲ The blunderbuss was used by many pirates.

But the Company stood no chance. The English king and many other governors were secretly sending their own privateers to fetch them some treasure. Many of the privateers settled on the island of Madagascar. From there, they sailed out to attack passing ships.

They planned their raids carefully. A ship going to India was usually filled with gold and silver. But a ship returning home was more often than not filled with spices or silk. Those cargoes were difficult to sell and did not fetch a lot of money.

Henry Avery and Captain Kidd
In 1695, a buccaneer called Henry Avery attacked two Muslim ships returning to India from Mecca.

◄ Swords like these were sharpened for battle.

One of the ships belonged to the Indian emperor. Its cargo was worth £325,000. The emperor was livid. Here was proof that the British were doing nothing to stamp out piracy. He threatened to stop all trade with Britain.

So a group of English businessmen in America sent a man after Avery. His name was Captain Kidd. The businessmen said he could keep a large share of the booty he took from the pirates.

◄ After his attack on the Indian ship, Henry Avery retired to England with his loot. But he was probably swindled out of it by merchants because he died penniless.

Kidd set out to capture Avery in 1696. Or at least that's what he said. He never caught Avery. Instead it seems that he turned pirate himself.

Kidd and his men attacked two merchant ships and escaped with £10,000 worth of booty. The Indian emperor was even more furious. To calm him down, Kidd was arrested the moment he returned to America.

On trial in England, Kidd admitted looting ships. But he insisted that it was his men who had made him do it. The crew denied that. They said Kidd had forced them to steal on pain of death.

◄ Some people believe that Kidd's treasure is guarded by the ghost of a dead pirate.

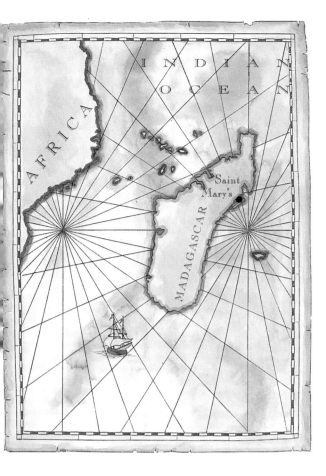

They even said that Kidd had buried a lot of treasure chests on Gardiner Island near New York City and along the Hudson River. The jury believed them. Kidd was hanged. His body was dipped in tar and hung in an iron cage at Tilbury Fort, in England.

It stayed there for many years, a grim reminder of what happens to pirates.

▲ Madagascar was a famous pirate haunt. Many of the buccaneers lived on the smaller island of Saint Mary's.

Kidd's treasure chests were never found, although many people have looked for them. Did they really exist or were the sailors lying to save their own skins? Perhaps no one will ever know.

► Hundreds of people turned out to watch Kidd being hanged.

Who were the Fiercest Pirates of the East?

A Boat load of Pi

For hundreds of years, Chinese and Japanese pirates attacked each other's ships. They also looted coastal towns and harbours.

In 1518, they were joined by a Portuguese pirate who built a fort near Macao in Southern China. From there he plundered passing ships. Three years later he was rooted out. But more European pirates followed. Many of them were respectable traders in disguise.

▼ The south China seas have been the home of the most ruthless pirates in the world.

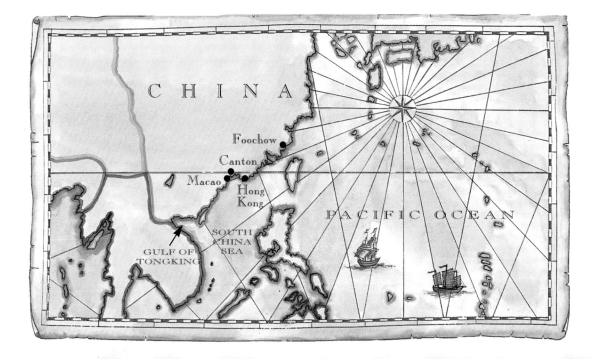

◄ Chinese people turned to piracy so they could have enough money to buy food.

Ching-Chi-ling

Ching-Chi-ling lived in the seventeenth century. He was one of the fiercest pirates in the East. His fleet of pirate ships, called junks, terrorised the Chinese coast all the way from Canton to the Yangtze River.

One day, Ching-Chi-ling was invited to work for the Tartars who had just invaded China. Immediately he travelled to Foochow, to take up his position. But the invitation was a trap. Ching was seized by the Tartars and thrown into prison. His ships were taken over by his son, Koxinga.

▼ Chinese pirates often used small junks fitted out with guns.

39

◄ Chinese pirates liked colourful flags that showed pictures of their captains.

When Ching-Chi-ling was beheaded, his pirates went on a rampage. All the people who lived on the Chinese coast had to be moved 20 km inland. Koxinga died in 1663. His son became captain in his place.

Ching Yih

No great pirate leader made his mark again until Ching Yih appeared in the nineteenth century. Ching Yih had 600 junks. They were divided into six fleets which attacked different parts of the coast. Some were lead by women pirates.

Each fleet had a main ship equipped with 12 guns and a supply of rowing boats. It also had its own flag.

► Ching Shih was not only a good fighter, she was also a brilliant accountant.

▼ The British built many streets like this in Hong Kong. Riches attracted pirates to the area.

Ching Shih

Ching Yih was killed during a tropical storm. His wife, Ching Shih, took over the fleet. She proved to be an even harsher pirate than her husband.

Ching Shih drew up a list of rules her pirates had to obey. No one could go ashore without permission. No man could abuse a woman. If someone wanted to marry a prisoner they had to buy her first.

Ching Shih was a brilliant pirate. She almost brought all the trade around China to a standstill. But in the end her fleet was weakened by in-fighting amongst the captains.

◀ One of Shap-'ng-tsai's junks goes up in smoke. It belonged to his lieutenant, Chui Apoo. The man escaped but his entire fleet was destroyed.

Ching Shih surrendered to the authorities in 1810. With her fleets weakened, she couldn't go on any longer. Some of her people were set free. They helped round up other pirates. Ching Shih herself disappeared. It is thought that she spent the rest of her days as a smuggler.

Shap-'ng-tsai

Thirty years later another famous pirate appeared. His name was Shap-'ng-tsai. His fleet attacked many coastal settlements. In 1849, the British and Chinese navies chased him 1,600 km across the sea.

▼ The British Navy destroys a fleet of pirate junks. In the foreground is a British paddle-steamer.

▲ The islands around Borneo were the home of the Balanini pirates. They used to capture people from the Philippines and sell them as slaves.

They cornered Shap-'ng-tsai in the Gulf of Tongking. By now the British had paddle-steamers. Shap-'ng-tsai's fleet didn't stand a chance. It was destroyed forever.

Malaccan Pirates

To reach China, European merchants had to pass through the Straits of Malacca, a canal between Sumatra and Malaysia. It was considered to be the most dangerous stretch of water in the world.

This statue shows Stamford Raffles. He not only founded a British colony in Singapore, he also discovered a rare flower called Rafflesia.

Many pirates operated in the Straits of Malacca. They hid in swamps and creeks. When a ship was sighted, they would creep upon it in small boats.

▼ Dyak pirates attack Rajah James Brooke's men. The Englishmen manage to sink one boat and kill the crew of the other.

Stamford Raffles

In 1819, an Englishman called Stamford Raffles set up a British settlement in Singapore. He vowed to destroy the pirates. The land for the settlement had been bought from a local ruler. Only the ruler was a pirate too. He had lots of spies who would inform him when a British ship was leaving harbour.

Rajah James Brooke and Henry Keppel

Another Englishman, Rajah James Brooke, decided to stamp out piracy too. Helped by a naval officer called Henry Keppel, he destroyed the bases of the Sariba pirates of Singapore. Then he wiped out the Dyaks who operated near Borneo. Soon other officers joined the fight.

One by one the pirate strongholds were destroyed. But piracy in the East was not completely wiped out. It still goes on to this very day. Traders beware!

▲ Sir Henry Keppel helped clear the seas of pirates around Borneo.

Who were the Bugi Men?

The Bugi men were trader pirates who plied the seas from New Guinea to Sumatra. They took slaves, raided settlements and attacked British ships. They were so feared that the word 'Bugiman' or 'Bogeyman' has come to mean a horrible creature.

Timeline

|| AD 1500 | 1650 | 1800 |

2000 BC

Phoenicians begin trading throughout Mediterranean

75 BC

Julius Caesar captured by pirates

67 BC

Pompey defeats Cilician pirates

1492

Christopher Columbus sails to America

1497

Vasco da Gama sails around Cape of Good Hope

1504

Aruj Barbarossa captures two of the Pope's ships

1516

Aruj Barbarossa dies

1523

Start of piracy in Caribbean

1530

Knights of St John move base to Malta

1543

Spanish treasure ships first sail in fleets

1570

Francis Drake's first privateering voyage

1601

First voyage of British East India Company

1630

Start of buccaneering in Caribbean

1661

Ching-Chi-ling beheaded

1670

Henry Morgan attacks Panama

1695

Henry Avery captures Moghul emperor's ship

1696

Captain Kidd sets out to capture Henry Avery

1701

Kidd hanged for piracy

1713

Treaty of Utrecht. Many sailors turn to piracy

1718

Death of Blackbeard

1720

Mary Read and Anne Bonny captured

1810

Ching Shih surrenders her pirate fleet

1830

Last corsairs in Mediterranean are rounded up

1849

Pirate fleets of Shap-'ng-tsai and Chui Apoo destroyed by British Navy

Glossary

Blunderbuss   A short large-bored gun.

Booty   Goods that are gained by fighting or plundering.

Coffer   A chest where valuables are kept.

Colonies   Countries belonging to foreign governments.

Deys   Local leaders of a Muslim country.

Galleon   A type of large ship used by the Spanish in the sixteenth century.

Gujurat   A region in India.

Junks   Chinese boats.

Lepanto   A harbour in Greece.

Maroon   To leave behind on a deserted island.

Pieces of eight   Old Spanish coins.

Plantation   A vast area of land used for growing crops.

Privateers   Pirates working with the permission of a government.

Ransom   To keep someone a prisoner until money is paid for their release.

Rhodes   An island in the Eastern Mediterranean.

Talents   Sums of money.

Further Information

Information books:

Eyewitness Guide: Pirate (Dorling Kindersley, 1995)

Films:

Peter Pan: Disney's famous cartoon about the wicked Captain Hook and the boy who refused to grow up.

Hook: Steven Spielberg's follow-up to the classic Peter Pan.

Shipwrecked: The story of a family captured by buccaneers.

The Goonies: A bunch of children go looking for buried treasure.

Index